MW01295571

Knowledge *is* Power

Car Stuff You Should Know

By

Russell McCloud

Knowledge *is* Power

Car Stuff You Should Know

Russell McCloud,
General Manager
Accurate Automotive Attention
1495 S. 3rd Avenue
Yuma, AZ 85364
928.783.8808
www.YumaCarCare.com

Paperback
Expert

www.PaperbackExpert.com

Permission to reproduce or transmit in any form or by any means, electronic or mechanical, including photocopying and recording, or by an information storage and retrieval system, must be obtained by contacting the author through his website.

ISBN-13: 978-1502567956

ISBN-10: 1502567954

This book is for educational purposes with the sole intent to educate the reader. By writing this book, the author is not giving legal advice. The author does not have any knowledge of the reader's specific situation; therefore readers should consult with a professional before acting on any of the information contained in this book. The author has taken reasonable precautions in the writing of this book and believes the facts presented in the book are accurate as of the date it was written. However, the author specifically disclaims any liability resulting from the use or application of the information in this book. If you need professional assistance, you should seek the services of a competent professional.

© Copyright 2014 by Russell McCloud   All Rights Reserved

First Printing: October 2014

❦❦❦❦❦❦

Dedication

This book is dedicated to the memory of my parents,
Dennis and Mary McCloud, whose hard work provided a lasting legacy
for their children and grandchildren.

Their faith was the foundation for our lives
and the business we continue in their honor.

I am eternally grateful for the legacy they left to me, my sisters and their
families, and to my two sons who have chosen to work in the family
business as well.

❦❦❦❦❦❦❦❦

Acknowledgements

I would like to acknowledge all those who have chosen to place their trust in our family's business over the years, allowing us to continue Dad's dream of providing automotive services to the Yuma community. Our family appreciates each of you who allows us the privilege of serving our community.

Of course, we could not provide this service without the great people who choose to work with us in the furtherance of our mission. We are richly blessed to have each of you with us.

Finally, my family members who keep it all going. My sister Michele and her husband Gene, Kim's husband John, and my two sons, Jeff & Scott, who have chosen to work in the family business. This would not be possible without each and every one of you. Thank you!

Testimonials/Customer Reviews

I want to say "Thank You!" to the many clients who choose to place their trust in us. If it weren't for them, we wouldn't have a job for our family members. Our clients are the people we appreciate the most and they deserve the highest acknowledgement.

Here's what a few of them have to say:

Since the early years of Accurate Automotive Attention, I have received professional service from the <u>entire</u> staff. George and Sheree, you have always rescued me—even with a short notice. To the Accurate Automotive Attention team, thank you for the attention that is given to your customers. - ***Dorothy L. Green***

I've used AAA for my car repairs for 12 years. I like the service and repair work on my cars. The office staff are very friendly and helpful. My girls also took their cars in for repair as needed. I feel as if they take care of my car like it is theirs. - ***Barbara DeBerry***

Russell McCloud and his team have been keeping my family and me safe and on the road for more than 30 years. His mechanics are knowledgeable, efficient, and tidy. George, Mitch, and Sheree are always helpful and friendly. Every time I take one of the many cars in my family's fleet, I know I'll be treated well. I can count on Accurate Automotive to provide the best service at a fair price. – ***Tim Chaulk***

Taking my car to Accurate Automotive Attention is like taking it to family. They have saved me time and money by providing preventative maintenance and only repairing what needs to be repaired. They look out for you, making repairs when they are minor before major work is needed. *Great business, fantastic customer service, and friendly people.* - **Steve Irr**

I've been doing business with you for over 38 years now. I know that you are going to do your best to solve any problem I bring to you. I feel very secure in coming to you for my car service. - **Dyan Witman**

Your staff are always the best. George, Mitch and Sheree are the greatest. We have been doing business with you since about 2002. – **Barbara & Charles Burgess**

Your service writer/customer care guy named "George" has influenced me more than anything else. When I bring a vehicle in, I am rarely rolling in bucks (never), and I am already predisposed to stress over the anticipated costs and interruption to my life. Even for scheduled events. They do cost money, and can include bad news.

George has always been cheerful and efficient. He always presents the reports of deficiencies for my vehicle to me in a way that I can understand well enough to set my OWN priorities when choosing the "what and when" to engage in. He never, ever hard sells me. (If you want me to leave, that's all you have to do. Because ALL hard sells are about the business and NOT about the customer.)

I have always received courteous treatment from the staff at AAA. The drivers giving me a needed ride while my vehicle is in repair, the down home friendly staff in the office are a couple of examples.

But the overarching reason that I come to AAA for vehicle service is that I know George will help me to design a care program from my vehicle. He helps me to design a program that is based upon my priorities. He is honest. He explains my vehicle's issues to me, but he also respects my decision making. - **Anella Crouch**

I've had really excellent service over the past 7 years from this organization. I highly recommend it to anyone who asks where I have my car serviced. I now have over 207,000 miles on my 1997 Toyota Camry and it runs like a charm! Have had the regular service recommendations done on it and I don't plan to buy a new car in the near future. This is due to the staff at Accurate Automotive! And the service is great—a ride to work and back when needed, too! – **Penny Myers**

In 1975 upon moving to Yuma from L.A, the truck needed service and some minor repairs. Not being familiar with any of the shops in Yuma, I asked several people for recommendations. Each person had a couple of ideas but one shop was on most of the lists—Accurate Automotive Attention owned by Dennis McCloud.

Taking a leap of faith, I went to AAA for the service and repair. The shop was neat, clean, the staff friendly with Mr. McCloud most welcoming. The Service Writer was a young (what could he know?) fair-

haired guy who wrote down everything I told him about the truck. He provided an estimate and when the work would be finished. The vehicle was finished on time and within the estimate provided by Russell. And I did not have an issue with the quality of the work or the cost. Only after the fact did I learn that the young guy was Dennis's son and had grown up in the business.

39 years later and that young kid Russell is the General Manager. The "Shop" is still neat, clean and the staff friendly and most accommodating. Thus it is: the vehicle goes in for service, the work is done correctly, and the vehicle comes out on time and within estimate. The services provided are top notch. I always recommend family and friends to Accurate Automotive Attention.

But the best part is that Russell is a friend. A friend involved in Yuma. A friend working to make Yuma ever better. A friend always with a smile. **- Richard I. Nicholls, Jr., 39 Year Yuma Resident**

Foreword

It will come as no surprise to friends of Russell McCloud that he has taken the time to write this book. The purpose of this work is to share his years of experience in the automotive industry with fellow car owners and enthusiasts to help them get the most out of car ownership. He has spent his career in automotive repair and has a lot of insight to share with car owners on how to avoid some major car problems.

I first met Russell in 1994, after moving to Yuma to operate an auto parts business. I wanted to be the best and of course, I wanted to do business with the best shops. Accurate Automotive Attention was at the top of my list. They were the largest and earned that position with innovation and attention to customer needs. I introduced myself to Russell's dad, Dennis McCloud. I asked him for his help in building my new business.

Dennis did help me by promising to consider me as a supplier, if I earned it. The first step was to be in business at the end of the year and prove to be a reliable supplier to an organization that relies on customer service. I spent the next year getting to know Accurate Automotive Attention and the McCloud family. They are an organization that keeps the customer needs in mind by investing in training for their technicians and investing in the best diagnostic equipment available.

Russell took the leadership of this business under the guidance of Dennis and continues the service and innovation that they are known for.

While his main focus in the family business was not hands-on repair, he took the training and became a Certified ASE Master Technician. It is this rich background that Russell has relied on to develop a guide for car owners.

The reader of this book will discover the information that is important in the maintenance of a vehicle. Russell even explains the "lingo" used in the automotive industry to help familiarize the car owner so they can have a more informed conversation with Service Advisors. This book answers questions on the dashboard lights and how to respond to your car's needs. Your car's owner's manual is obviously helpful, but the practical knowledge of someone who has handled these repair questions for years takes the mystery out of a strange light or gauge instructing you to do something.

It is impressive to me that Russell wrote this book so that the reader can avoid the repair shop. It is a testament to him and to his attitude towards customer satisfaction. He covers many of the customer complaints about vehicles that he has heard over the years. These complaints range from strange noises and what they could mean to routine maintenance items that an owner can check themselves. All of this is shared in an effort to lower the cost of ownership by understanding the basics of your car's systems.

All mechanical systems, including those on your car, are eventually going to wear or malfunction. Relying on a professional is inevitable. Russell gives solid advice on choosing a repair facility and he also discusses how to deal with a Service Advisor or shop owner in handling a situation that has gone wrong. This book covers all aspects of owning a car from buying it, to changing a flat. I recommend it to any car owner and will make sure my kids get a copy.

Russell T. Clark
Yuma County Supervisor, District #3

Table of Contents

CHAPTER

I

WHY I WROTE THIS BOOK

Designed to replace the horse, the automobile was originally called the "horseless carriage." It has succeeded in its original goals, getting us where we want to go faster than horses ever could and making our work much easier.

I remember when each car seemed to take on the owner's personality. And when a car was coming toward you, you knew exactly what make and model it was—there weren't that many possibilities! Certainly nowhere near the many different nameplates and hundreds of different models we have now, made even more difficult by the number of years cars stay on the road these days.

Technology advances so rapidly now that a complete understanding of your car is nearly impossible. People tell me they used to be able to look under the hood and name every part they saw. Today some of those same people won't even raise the hood since virtually nothing is recognizable! Most of my clients admit they'd love to know more about their cars and learn how to save money on their transportation investment. That's why I wrote this book.

I see a need for people to know not only how to take care of their car but to acquire wisdom they can use when they replace it with a new or used one. So here it is—the self-help book of car ownership. It won't make you a Master Certified auto technician, but it will help you better understand how to keep yourself, your family, and your car safe.

Safety is a primary objective every time we get in a car. We pray for travel mercies. We tell our children to drive safely. Road signs tell us to drive safely, to wear our seat belts, and obey traffic laws—all so that we will "arrive alive" at our destinations.

Cars were never meant to be phone booths, texting stations or music halls. They were meant to help us arrive conveniently and safely. Most of the advancements in technology have an underlying theme of safety, many of which are addressed in these pages. More importantly, this book provides simple, helpful information on car ownership. Armed with this knowledge, understanding the warning signs, and knowing what to do when things go wrong will help you stay safer in and around your automobiles.

With this book, I hope to reach out to my current client base to help them become more informed about their vehicles. However, they are already talking to my Service Advisors who do a great job of communicating with them, so for many of them this book is simply supplementing that information. My greater ambition is to expand my reach to other drivers, especially new drivers and new car owners so they can gain insight into the reasons for, and importance of, maintaining their vehicles. Additionally, I want to equip readers with the information they need to find a car care shop they can trust for ethical treatment, great workmanship and fabulous warranties.

So, consider me the "car guy dad you never had" who desires you to know how to care for your car and arrive safely. If you have a specific question, simply go to YumaCarCare.com. If you do not find what you are looking for there, please call me at 928.783.8808 and let me know how I can help.

Sincerely,

Russell McCloud, AAM
General Manager
Accurate Automotive Attention
September 2014

www.YumaCarCare.com

CHAPTER

2

HISTORY: OUR BUSINESS, OUR FAMILY

If you read the dedication to this book, you know I'm very grateful to my parents for starting this company on October 29, 1969. Both my parents were smart, hardworking people. My mother was the driving force behind Yuma Title & Trust, a two-person operation in the beginning that eventually became the largest and best-known title company in Yuma (since purchased by Chicago Title). Dad's dream was to own and operate an automotive repair company. He achieved that dream with the company they named *Accurate Automotive Attention*.

When my father founded the company, he had exactly zero customers. It was a brave step. Accompanied by one mechanic's helper, he set up shop in a small, rented metal building on the corner of 15th Street and 3rd Avenue.

The first person through the door was Jack Culver, who owned Culver Refrigeration, located half a block down the street. Jack brought

in his 1962 Chevrolet pickup truck and was our first customer. Believe it or not, that truck is still running. It's been through several owners, but they've all kept it well maintained. We've known all three owners, and even though it wasn't always serviced here, we're happy to take part of the credit for it still being on the road.

With customers like Jack, Dad was able to add a 6,000 square foot addition and stucco the metal building in 1971. By then, I was working summers and part time after school for a whopping 40 cents an hour. (The federal minimum wage in those days was $1.60. I guess he figured he made up the rest by feeding me, keeping a roof over my head—all that other stuff parents do.) Dad kept me busy sweeping and mopping floors, running parts, and generally helping out. Thanks to his dedication to quality and service, his business continued to grow.

Our community was growing, too. That growth meant even more business for Accurate Automotive Attention. Only three years later, Dad added another 5,300 square feet to the business, expanding to the limits of his property. Under Dad's leadership, applying the same principles of integrity, quality and service, Accurate Automotive Attention continued to grow and prosper. During this time Dad had me running his machine shop. Since it was precision work and not the same type of work as a general technician performs, I was pretty good at it. Somehow that natural talent with tools just didn't filter down to me.

6

In 1984, we saw a need for quality auto care in the unincorporated area east of Yuma, known as The Foothills, to service the growing population in that area. To meet that need, we expanded by adding a small facility at 12543 S. Frontage Road. By this time, Dad had hired a "real" machinist and had me doing Service Advisor work. Thankfully, I was better at working with people than I was at mechanical work. Dad had also acquired a tow truck and I became the part time tow driver along with my sister Michele who also filled that role from time to time.

In 1986, we were well on our way to becoming a full-service automotive care company. That's when we became the AAA Arizona towing contractor for the Yuma area and expanded our tow truck service to two full time drivers. Today we run five full time employees for these services, operating four tow trucks and one battery service truck.

By 1992, our facilities had reached their capacities as the community and our customer base continued to grow. Fortunately, in late 1995 we were able to purchase a building and three adjacent lots north of our 3rd Avenue location. We also purchased another 12,800 square feet of building on the east side of 3rd Avenue and moved our diagnostic team there, creating a separate tune-up and diagnostic facility. This brought our total "under roof" square footage to almost 33,000 square feet. Over time, that diagnostic facility turned into indoor parking and vehicle storage due to the increased reliability of electronic engine systems.

In July of 1998, Accurate Automotive Attention again branched out into the Foothills community by purchasing a modern quick service facility that included a car wash and RV wash facility. The RV wash facility is the only one of its kind in Arizona. We named this facility *Express* Auto/RV Care Center. This expansion added eleven dedicated

7

employees and provided another valuable service to this area. Since purchasing the facility, we have added detailing services and now have 25 employees at that location.

It was about his time that I stepped away from the front counter, letting others handle that job better than I did. I began taking on more responsibility and working more as an owner instead of an employee. Any of our Service Advisors will tell you that the farther away from the front counter I am, the better things go.

Companywide, we now employ at least 40 and up to 48 employees during the year, depending on seasonal fluctuations. So, from that single shop, we've become a conglomerate. Well, not exactly, but we've certainly expanded beyond anything Dad imagined back in 1969. Now, we are truly a full-service automotive care company.

Do you need your car detailed? We've got you covered. Is your battery dead? Got it. Locked out? Had an accident? Need a tune-up? Does your RV need a wash? Are your brakes grinding? Whatever your automotive issue, you can call us. We'll take care of you and do our best to solve your problem; we'll help you out, just as my Dad envisioned when he started this company back in 1969.

Sadly, we lost our founder, my Dad, Dennis McCloud, in November 2006. We—his children and grandchildren—are committed to carrying on his legacy into the third generation and beyond. To illustrate that commitment, I'd like to tell you a little more about who we are and explain what I mean when I say we are a family-owned and run business. I'm not simply talking about a business that has one or two family members with "token" jobs or titles.

My sister, Michele, handles the financial matters for all three locations. Her husband, Gene, is a brilliant technician who works with us at the original location. Whenever there's a problem that has everyone else stumped, Gene gets involved and always finds a solution.

My other brother-in-law, John, runs the *Express* Auto and RV Care Center. My son Jeff, who was trained by Gene when he was still a teenager, works at that location with John. I'm very proud of Jeff, who is an extremely talented and expert electronics and electrical diagnostician and technician. He's also a whiz at diesels. We assume he inherited my father's mechanical skills—they definitely skipped past me. I picked up a lot of knowledge about cars through my years in the industry, but I've never actually done the mechanical repair work. I've been blessed in finding and keeping some of the best mechanics in the business—including Jeff.

Jeff's wife, Brianne, works at the Foothills Frontage Road location. She joined the company in 2013 and we are pleased to have her working with us.

My son Scott helps to manage the day-to-day operations of our towing division, Accurate Towing. He has a broad knowledge of the towing operation and is an invaluable part of that division.

As you can see, we have family members at every location and in all phases of the operations. Everyone in our family is dedicated to carrying on in the Christian tradition of integrity, quality and exceptional service my dad brought to this industry when he founded *Accurate Automotive Attention*.

CHAPTER

3

MY STORY: HOW DID I GET HERE?

How *did* I get here? I didn't plan to work for my father or go into the automotive business. I was going to be a nuclear engineer or a marine biologist. (That's right; I was seriously considering trading the desert for the ocean!) But things didn't quite work out according to my plans.

Believe me, I'm glad things turned out this way. I'm a happy man who loves his work and I'm exactly where I want to be. It's just not what I expected when I was planning my future.

When I was about twelve years old, I started doing little jobs around the shop. Doing things like sweeping the floors and keeping the shop tidy, being a "gofer" and running parts. I learned to ride my bike for about a mile with no hands—I had to. My hands were full of parts!

I continued working like that—on a part-time basis, strictly as a temporary thing—until I graduated high school. Then I went to college. When I came home after my first semester, Dad told me he wanted to buy some machine equipment and asked me to run the machine shop.

I thought it would be a nice break from college. I'd take a year off, do my dad a favor, manage the machine shop and then get back with the program. I'd finish studying to be a scientist of some description.

Since I'm still here, I definitely wound up staying a little more than a year! I met a young lady, got married, had a family and one thing led to another. But I'm skipping ahead, so let me go back.

When I was about 25, Dad asked me to start running the shop as the Service Advisor. My job would be greeting the clients, dispatching the work and road testing vehicles. He would stick to managing the paperwork. Of course, if there were any problems, he was available to help resolve them. It was fortunate for the company that he was there, because that was not my forte.

There were a few issues once I started in my new role. One of our employees quit because he wasn't going to take orders from "a little kid." However, most of the employees were fine with it and I did a pretty good job.

I continued running the shop that way for about 18 years, although I hired some help as technology kept advancing and cars became more complicated. Today, Service Advisors have to spend time with clients and it takes time to put together an estimate. Back when I started, you could look at a car, see what was wrong and write an estimate based on experience. Those days are long gone.

Eventually I hired someone to help with the workload, was able to attend more training and came to realize that I probably shouldn't be doing that job at all! I discovered I had a lot to learn about the best practices in running an automotive shop and that I should be focusing my efforts there, helping my dad make our shop better—better for the customers, the employees and for us, the owners. So, understanding that, I eventually transitioned away from working one-on-one with our clients every day and began hiring Service Advisors who could do a better job than I could.

So now, I'm the General Manager, with the final responsibility for all our operations. As you read in the previous section, we've come a long way from the single shop my dad originally started, where I started out sweeping floors. I have to say my job is the best gig in the world—everyone else does all the work and I get all the credit. It's hard to beat that!

Seriously, I understand how richly blessed I am. I am grateful each day for the many blessings in my life.

www.YumaCarCare.com

CHAPTER

4

ACCURATE AUTOMOTIVE
ATTENTION TODAY

People think we fix cars for a living here at Accurate Automotive Attention. But, that's not what we really do. What we actually do is solve problems for our clients. You depend on your car, and if it isn't performing well, you have a problem. We solve that problem for you.

Cars are notoriously bad investments. How many times have you heard someone comment on the loss of value in a car "the minute it's driven off the showroom floor?" Cars are usually the second largest investment you make, next to your home. You expect your home to gain in value over time. What about that investment in your car?

We can help you make the most of that investment. We try to establish long-term relationships with our clients, to work with them and protect that investment by meeting their goals for their vehicle, whether it's to extend the vehicle's life as long as possible or simply to keep it in good running order until it's time to trade.

We know we're successful in building those long-term relationships and making our customers happy. What's the proof? Obviously, for one thing, all the repeat business we get. But, you wouldn't believe how often our clients stop by with a batch of cookies or a cake, or drop in to introduce their pet. Or, sometimes simply stop by to say hello because they were in the neighborhood.

We enjoy our relationships with our clients, especially the ones who bring treats. Just kidding about the treats! (Sort of.) Every client is important to us. We love building new relationships and we're incredibly grateful for our long-term relationships.

Awards

We also know we're doing something right because we've been voted "Yuma's Best" by readers of *The Sun* 14 times. We have been awarded AAA Arizona's "Top Shop" award four times, most recently in 2012.

The true professionals, the people who come to work for us every day and do such a great job working with our clients and on their vehicles, solving their problems—we would be nothing without them. I appreciate my staff—their hard work, their commitment to our company and to the ASA Code of Ethics.

AUTOMOTIVE SERVICES ASSOCIATION (ASA)

The Automotive Service Association (ASA) is a 60-year old nonprofit organization that advances professionalism and excellence in the automotive repair industry. The ASA provides education, representation and member services. It is the leading organization for owners and managers of automotive service businesses striving to deliver excellence in service and repairs to consumers[i].

We are proud members of the ASA. My involvement with the ASA started in the late 1990's and, almost by accident, I was asked by the state director to take over the local chapter. Since then, I've been honored to serve on the state and national levels of the ASA (details provided in the *About the Author* section of this book.) Please look at *Appendix II* to see the ASA Code of Ethics that guides all our business transactions and decisions.

Another extremely important result of that involvement was that I began taking management courses and discovered how much I didn't know. Before that, I had no idea how little I knew! That training has been invaluable to our company and is probably the reason our company is still thriving today. I am forever grateful to ASA for that shop owner training. It helps us run our shops better and do a better job of caring for our clients and solving their problems.

WARRANTIES

Our basic warranty is for 24 months or 24,000 miles with rare exceptions on parts. For anything else we install, we'll apply a three-year, 36,000-mile warranty to it if you can bring it back to us. If you're

17

traveling, don't worry, our 24 month, 24,000 mile warranty follows you nationwide.

That nationwide warranty can be a real lifesaver. If you're traveling across country and something we installed fails in that 2-year period, you can contact us, give us the zip code for your current area, and we'll do the research to find a good shop in that area. We'll call that shop, explain the problem, give them your history and the repair history of your vehicle and set up the process to get your car repaired. We'll do everything we can to make that process as easy, painless and quick as possible for you. Using this warranty process will not cost you additional repair expense if the problem was related to work we did that's covered under our extensive warranty program.

New Car Maintenance

Sometimes clients tell us they've purchased a new car so they won't be seeing us for a while. The salesperson told them they'd void their warranty if they didn't have their vehicle serviced by the dealer while it was under warranty.

Wrong. Maybe they misunderstood what the salesperson said. The truth is that you can even perform your own oil changes without voiding your warranty *as long as you keep records of that maintenance.*

If you perform an oil change, you need to keep the receipts for the oil and the filter. If we perform your maintenance, we keep those records for you. That means, even if you're traveling and have an issue, we can produce those records and send them directly to the company, right away.

Not only does our record-keeping come in handy in situations where you need to prove your vehicle has been well-maintained, including when you're ready to sell or trade it, but it allows us to remind you when it's time for service. That takes one routine item off your mind and frees you to attend to other important matters in your busy schedule.

CHAPTER

5

CAR CARE 101

LEARNING THE LINGO: ACRONYMS

Communication can easily break down in my industry due to the many acronyms we use. Listed here are some of the most common ones. I hope these will provide you with a knowledge base to help you make informed decisions about keeping your vehicle serviced properly.

LOF = Lube, Oil and Filter Service

LOF is pronounced "loaf." What's a "loaf?" In our industry, 'LOF' means Lube, Oil and Filter. Interestingly enough, not a lot of cars receive lubrication anymore, but the acronym has carried over for many years. So, if you see the term "LOF," that refers to an oil change on a vehicle. If you hear your Service Advisor handing your car off to a tech and telling them they have a "loaf," do not think they have been told to goof off on your car.

ABS = Anti-Lock Brake System

If you read that as a word, it says "abs." So, if we were a gym, you would think of something totally different—one part of your body. But in the car industry, ABS is an acronym for Anti-lock Brake System. So, if your "ABS" light comes on, that means there's a fault in the Anti-lock Brake System. If the "ABS" light is on, an important safety system is not working properly!

DIS = Driver Information System

This is the vehicle's system that provides information to the driver. It may be an LED-type style, a warning light in the console, scrolling across the dash or touch screen, or perhaps visible in a small window somewhere on the dash. You need to be aware of this important system. Pay close attention to any message and look for more specific information in the index of your owner's manual.

ASE = Automotive Service Excellence

You'll see this one a lot. ASE is an independent organization that tests the competency of those in our industry. ASE does not do training; they only do testing for competency. The training takes place in another location or through other venues, much like a student taking the SAT exam. It's administered at a testing location under close supervision and the results are provided by the certifying organization. Almost all of our technicians are ASE certified and those that are not yet will be soon. We are proud to grow our own young technicians and after they have received adequate experience, we will encourage them to obtain their ASE certifications to improve their resume.

ASE says, "We're going to see if you learned anything through what you have studied. If you can pass our test, then we will certify that you know what you are talking about and are qualified to repair these specific systems." When someone passes their exam, they become "ASE Certified." For the automotive repair side of our industry, there are eight different areas of ASE certification. If you are certified in all eight, you are an ASE Master Technician.

ASE also has specific certifications for people working in a parts department and certifications for Service Advisors. Our Parts Manager and Service Advisors have these certifications and are proud of their accomplishments.

ASE is the "gold standard" in our industry, and in my opinion, it is important that any company you choose to work on your vehicle should employ ASE Certified technicians. Before you have any work done on your vehicle, ask if the company employs ASE Certified technicians and Service Advisors. If they don't, you may want to look for a repair shop with fully trained and certified technicians and Service Advisors.

An ASE Certification has to be renewed every five years. This is important because cars and technology change. Therefore, ASE Certified Technicians must stay up to date on cutting-edge technology so they can continue to service your vehicles properly. Every year there are over a million pages of new information hitting our industry, so it's important for my staff and me to stay current.

Your great-grandfather may have said all he needed to fix his car was a piece of baling wire, a pair of pliers and some duct tape. That may have been true back then, but today, we need a little more than that. That is why being ASE Certified is so important.

TPMS = Tire Pressure Monitoring System

TPMS stands for Tire Pressure Monitoring System. Like the name says, this system monitors the tire pressure of your car. After Ford had problems with accidents caused by low air pressure on their vehicles' tires, the federal government mandated that all vehicles, beginning in 2008-2009, must contain a Tire Pressure Monitoring System.

Today, the technology actually notifies the driver when a tire has low pressure. Some systems will tell you about a specific tire—for instance, "your left front tire is low." Some simply indicate that you have a low tire somewhere on the vehicle. Spare tires also have these sensors—so although the four tires on the ground may be fine, you should still check the spare tire as well.

EGR = Exhaust Gas Recirculation

EGR is an acronym you'll hear often. It stands for Exhaust Gas Recirculation. It is an emission control item and a system that recirculates exhaust gases back into the engine for re-burning. This slows the burn process by diluting the air-fuel ratio to avoid what you may know as "pinging," a destructive and noisy occurrence that's most noticeable on acceleration. The ultimate purpose of EGR is to reduce the emission of oxides of nitrogen, which are harmful and pollutant gases.

APP = Accelerator Pedal Position (Sensor)

In the past, a car had a physical cable that connected the gas pedal with the throttle control mechanism on the engine. Today, instead of a cable, your vehicle uses an accelerator position sensor, which means that your gas pedal is now an electronic sensor. When you push down on the gas pedal, you are moving a very high tech sensor. The gas pedal sensor information is sent to the onboard computer (PCM) which then computes how much fuel and air to allow into the engine.

TPS = Throttle Position Sensor

This sensor is attached to the actual throttle plate on the engine, which controls the amount of air allowed to enter, thereby controlling the speed and power production of the engine. Because modern engines are "throttle by wire," meaning there is no mechanical connection between the accelerator pedal and throttle, this sensor is a critical input to the computer. In fact, most vehicles are equipped with a complex TPS, which actually has multiple position sensors built into it for redundancy.

PCM = Powertrain Control Module

The PCM is the grandfather of the computer systems on the vehicle. It is the mission control center, the head honcho, the boss—it is what everything else goes through. Typically, there are many computers within a single car and they all communicate with the PCM.

BCM = Body Control Module

The Body Control Module pays attention to everything internal (inside the vehicle). "Things you touch" is a simple way to define what goes through the BCM—for example, turn signals, headlights, heating and air conditioning controls and other items like these. They all send information through the Body Control Module.

AT = Automatic Transmission

This is the type of transmission in most passenger vehicles. In fact, it's increasingly difficult to find a standard transmission anymore. If your gearshift has choices like "Park," "Reverse" and "Drive," you have an automatic transmission. This type of transmission automatically shifts when certain conditions exist.

The invention of the automatic transmission revolutionized the driving of vehicles, making it much easier to learn to drive. Before this time, drivers had to use a clutch pedal and manually shift their car into different gears. That's why it's called a "manual" or standard transmission.

DASHBOARD: LIGHTS THAT POP UP

As you sit in the driver's seat and turn on the key, you see various lights pop up on the dashboard. But what do they mean?

First, there's a reason for the color of lights on your dashboard. These colors can be associated with the traffic lights you see when you are driving down the road.

If you see a RED light, what does that usually mean to you? Stop. And when you see YELLOW? Caution. GREEN? Green means go.

Let's apply this to the dashboard lights. If, for example, you have the cruise control on, the button is normally some sort of orange color. Once you set the cruise control, the button turns green.

Your dashboard lights are very important and should never be ignored. If one of your red dashboard lights comes on, you need to seek service by a qualified technician right away. You typically should discontinue driving immediately.

ABS Light:

The ABS light has to do with the brakes, as we mentioned previously. If the ABS light is on, the Anti-lock Brake System computer has found a fault somewhere in the system. It could be anything from low brake fluid to a problem with a particular wheel sensor or another component within the system.

When the ABS light is on, your normal braking will still work. However, if you get into a panic stop, the anti-lock brake system will *not* take over your braking—that is, your wheels will lock up like a vehicle not equipped with anti-lock brakes. Therefore, you lose the ability to maneuver around objects in your path. Instead, momentum carries you forward and you'll likely hit the object ahead of you.

You may remember your parents telling you that if you're on ice you should pump your brakes and not apply them hard. The ABS System uses that principle as well. The ABS system pumps your brakes ten times per second, which is something no human is able to do.

The ABS light typically comes on as a yellow light. It doesn't mean that you have to immediately stop the car, but it does indicate that the system is not going to work until you get it resolved. It does not mean

27

that your car won't stop; it does not mean that your brakes have failed completely; it only means that the anti-lock side of your brake system is not going to operate if you get into a panic stop situation or trying to stop on a slick surface. Drive cautiously—as you always should—and quickly get your vehicle to a shop for testing.

Check Engine Light:

The check engine light has been around since about 1990. Its initial purpose was to provide information about the emission control status of the vehicle. Check engine lights are typically orange in color because they still primarily deal with emission controls. However, emission controls now includes additional elements, as well.

Emissions concern air pollution—so, for instance, if a spark plug is not working properly, it causes the car to pollute more than it should, and the check engine light comes on.

Formerly, a failed spark plug wouldn't cause the check engine light to come on. It would come on if you had a fuel canister that was full of gasoline or if the EGR (Exhaust Gas Recirculation) system failed. Now the check engine light encompasses many things. There are somewhere between six hundred and nine hundred different reasons why the check engine light might come on. A technician needs to run tests on the system to determine the actual cause so they can correct this problem.

SRS Light:

Air bags are very important. In a car equipped with air bags you will see an SRS light (or Air Bag light) on the dashboard. SRS is an acronym for Supplementary Restraint System—the key word being *supplementary*.

That means it supplements your safety system and that safety system is your seat belt. If you are not wearing your seat belt when you are in an accident that deploys the airbags, a greater amount of bodily injury will occur. For that reason, *you should ALWAYS wear your seatbelt.*

If the airbag light is on, there is a problem in the system and the airbags will not deploy if an accident occurs. As you can imagine, this can be very serious. If your SRS light comes on, get your vehicle to the shop quickly.

Traction Control Light:

The vehicle computer not only monitors the brake system and airbags, but it also helps move power from one tire to another in all-wheel-drive vehicles. For example, in an all-wheel drive vehicle, let's say you become stuck in sand, mud, ice or snow and are trying to get out. One of your wheels is usually stuck worse than the others—it's spinning but not getting any traction. The traction control system will move the power from the wheel that is spinning to a wheel that is not since the non-spinning wheel has greater traction. The traction control system allows power to be transferred so that you can gain traction, have greater control and get out of a situation where you may normally remain stuck.

Traction control also works during acceleration. An example of acceleration mode is when you turn a corner and the weight of the car shifts from one side to the other. The traction control system is going to move the power to the wheels with the best traction.

29

The traction control light comes on momentarily whenever the system activates. If there's a failure in the system, the light will stay on. That is when you need to take your vehicle in for inspection.

Reduced Power Light:

Reduced power is something primarily seen on GM vehicles. The reduced power light is usually red and indicates that something has gone wrong, that the vehicle has gone into "limp mode"—as in "we are limping" or "we only have one leg and cannot run." Such a fault in this system could be problematic. Many times, this fault pertains to either transmission functions or accelerating functions. If this light comes on, you must get it in for service.

Some limp modes limit your speed to no more than 25 miles an hour, which will allow you to drive to a safe place. You'll likely need to have it towed from that point, especially if you have a long way to go. Other limp modes allow you to go 40 miles per hour, usually enough that you can get to a repair facility on your own.

The reduced power light will almost always be red. It indicates a problem that needs to receive immediate attention.

Temperature Light:

Most cars today have an engine temperature gauge as well as a temperature light. The engine temperature light will always be red, indicating that you need to shut the car down as soon as possible. The longer you continue to drive, the more damage will occur. Eventually, you will damage the engine internally. By continuing to drive the vehicle you will create more problems—very costly problems.

When the temperature light comes on, you should pull over and check the temperature gauge. If it indicates the engine is too hot, turn your vehicle off as quickly as you safely can. The first step in the troubleshooting process is to make sure that your coolant level is full. However, be very careful!

You have to use extreme caution when checking your coolant level or adding coolant to a hot car because you can be burned. It is best to let the car sit for at least an hour, with the hood raised, to cool down before adding coolant. You must check the radiator coolant level, not just the overflow bottle.

The need to add coolant usually indicates you have a leak that needs to be repaired. If the coolant is full and the vehicle is running hot, that means that a component within the system has failed. Either way, you'll need to get your car to the repair facility quickly.

Oil Light:

The oil light can indicate an issue with the oil level or oil pressure—sometimes both. If the engine loses oil pressure, the oil light is going to come on. That light will be red because you have to shut the engine down quickly. If the oil pressure is too low, there will be internal damage to the engine. The damage would be similar to driving without oil in the engine.

To clarify, you can be low on oil and still have oil pressure. The oil light may not let you know that you are low on oil—in some cars, only checking the level with a dipstick can tell you if you are low on oil. (One new technology in some of the higher end cars, like some BMW and Mercedes models, uses no dipstick. Instead, a sensor inside the

31

engine reads the oil level and indicates its level. Most cars still have a dipstick.)

Even when you're a quart or two low on oil, you still have enough oil in the engine to produce oil pressure. In that case, the oil light might not come on because adequate oil pressure exists. However, the lower your oil level, the more stress and damage to your engine may occur. Potentially, you could have a low oil level and no indicator light to warn you. That's why regular oil changes are so important.

Having a sufficient oil level provides several benefits. Lubricating the engine is the oil's primary job, but it also assists in engine cooling and increases fuel mileage when the proper oil is used.

Smart Air Bag Light:

Almost all cars are equipped with smart air bags. These sensors measure the weight of the person in the front passenger seat. Depending on the weight of the person or object in that seat, the air bag may or may not deploy. With this light, there is nothing you need to do. If there is a small child in the front seat, the smart bag knows it. If the weight in the front seat does not meet a certain criteria established by the manufacturer, the smart air bag light will come on to let you know that the airbag is off on the passenger side.

The reason the airbag doesn't deploy with a child in the front passenger seat is because the car industry has learned that small children do not withstand the explosion of an airbag as well as an adult.

The inside of an airbag contains a substance similar to gunpowder. When triggered, the "gunpowder" explodes the bag out of the dash at an extremely high rate of speed. The air inside that bag immediately deflates, but is present for just long enough to provide a cushion to the blow of an impact.

Typically, the occupant of the seat moves forward while the bag deploys rearward so a collision takes place between the bag and the occupant. Because the airbag deploys at such a high rate of speed, a child's body simply cannot withstand that kind of force. Injury or death can occur as a result. After learning this, car manufacturers introduced smart bags—which was quite a "smart" thing to do.

DASHBOARD GAUGES

Many cars have dashboard gauges in addition to dashboard lights. The following are the primary gauges you'll find on the dashboards of today's vehicles. They allow us a quick and easy way to tell how well our car is functioning.

Temperature Gauge:

One common gauge is the cold/hot gauge, also referred to as the coolant temperature gauge.

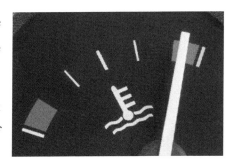

Typically, you find the coolant temperature gauge on the left side of the dash. This gauge monitors the temperature of the engine.

Transmissions usually will not shift into the final drive gear until the engine temperature has reached at least a quarter of the way of its full gauge range. Most gauges are set to run—in normal operation—about midway up the gauge. So, you'll usually see a "C" (for cold) on the bottom and an "H" (for hot) on the top (or Blue for cold and Red for hot).

The gauge could be installed horizontally—in that case, the 'C' would be on the left and the 'H' would be on the right. The needle is typically going to be in the middle of the gauge, indicating what is called, "Normal Operating Temperature."

Interestingly, if the indicator needle indicates your engine is staying cold, that impacts your fuel mileage. The vehicle's computer is designed to put fuel in the engine based on a certain engine temperature. When the engine is cold, it puts in more fuel because a cold engine needs more. If the thermostat is not working—a typical failure—then the computer perceives that the engine is running at a colder temperature and continues putting more fuel into the engine, increasing your gasoline usage. Because the thermostat can affect fuel mileage, it's important that

34

you are familiar with the temperature gauge to know what is normal. Check that gauge on a consistent basis.

> **Note:** If you continue running the vehicle when the gauge shows the engine is hot, this will cause *very expensive and critical internal engine damage*. Too many times we have seen very expensive engine damage caused by someone who knew the gauge was reading hot but explained that they only drove "less than a mile" to get to an exit, home, or elsewhere. *Don't make this mistake!*

Tachometer:

Most tachometer gauges (also called "tachs" or RPM gauges) are circular and have a series of numbers on them—often 0-8.

Even if you are sitting still, you will see the tachometer needle move around the gauge as you accelerate by pressing on the gas pedal. The tachometer indicates how many times the engine is rotating each minute. Multiply the number on the gauge by one thousand—for example, if the needle is sitting at 1, the engine is rotating one thousand times per minute. (If the numbers on the tachometer are multiples of 10—numbers like 20, 30, 40, and so on—then you multiply that number by one hundred instead of one thousand.) That number is how many times the engine makes one full revolution each minute—called revolutions per minute or "RPMs" for short.

It can be helpful to keep an eye on the RPM gauge. The RPM number will drop each time the transmission shifts into a higher gear to increase fuel economy. If you notice that the engine appears to be running at a higher RPM than normal, it may indicate that something is not right—that the engine is working harder than usual. Another situation when the tachometer is helpful is as you are idling. If you have a vacuum leak or a similar problem, your idling RPM will be higher than usual. Most engines should run just below the 1 mark. If the idling RPM is significantly higher, that's a problem. You should expect to see the idling RPM a little bit higher when the engine is cold. Once the engine reaches operating temperature, you will see the gauge go back down to the 650-750 RPM range. Isn't understanding acronyms cool?

Battery Gauge:

The battery gauge, also known as the "voltage gauge", simply measures battery voltage, and you will usually see a small picture of a battery on this gauge. Some gauges will have a number 12, which relates to the voltage; however, most of the time the normal position for the needle, when everything is fine with the battery and charging system, is in the middle of the gauge.

Fuel Gauge:

Most people know that "E" does not stand for "enough"—it stands for empty. And "F," of course, stands for full.

In today's cars, the fuel pump is located *inside* the gas tank. Having enough fuel in the tank helps keep that little electric motor—called your fuel pump—cool, and will typically make it last longer.

As a rule, you should keep at least a quarter tank of fuel in your car at all times. This will add life to the fuel pump because it is an electric motor which creates heat while running. Excessive heat shortens the life of the pump. That's why keeping enough fuel in the tank helps it last longer, especially in the Yuma climate.

My advice is to refuel your car completely when your gauge indicates a quarter of a tank. If you always run in that quarter to empty range, you're going to shorten the life of the pump and that is an expensive repair. Not only that, but when you need to get somewhere right away, you will want more than a quarter of a tank of gas.

Odometer:

The odometer gauge tells you how many miles are on your vehicle. The accuracy of an odometer gauge has changed over the years. Today it's electronic, whereas years ago, a cable ran from the speedometer head down to the transmission. As the transmission rotated, this cable rotated. Because of that, odometer readings could be altered. That's impossible with the LED-displayed odometers we have today. The odometer gauge accurately shows how many miles are on a car.

Speedometer:

The speedometer gauge shows how fast you are moving using reliable and accurate speed sensors. The onboard computer also uses this information to tell the transmission when to shift.

NOISES

One of the greatest things about car ownership is really getting to know your car. That means using your five senses—hearing, sight, smell, taste, and touch. You can use your senses to know what is normal for *your* car so you'll recognize when something has changed.

When it comes to hearing noises that you know are not normal—not what you are used to hearing—one of the best things to do is "show the noise."

When you take the car into a service facility, don't try to explain the noise. *Show* them the noise. One of the greatest helps to any service facility is when the vehicle owner pays attention so they can duplicate the noise.

- How fast was I going?
- Was I turning?
- Was I braking?
- Was I accelerating?
- What were the scenarios?
- Was I going uphill or downhill?

Pay attention to the environment and the activity that is taking place when the noise occurs. Then you can take that information, go to the repair facility, get someone in the car with you and duplicate the sound. Highly trained automotive technicians can typically hear many noises that you may not hear. This small step will assist the technician in locating and correcting the same noise that concerned you. When you pay attention to how the car normally sounds, you'll recognize when something changes.

Brake Squeaking

One common noise that often scares people is a squeaky noise that happens when you push on your brake pedal. A high-pitched noise is indicative of brakes needing repair, especially if this is a new sound. Sometimes what we'll call "inferior" brake pads or "inferior" parts are used on a brake job. In those cases, you should expect some squeaking.

The sound is not necessarily metal contacting metal, but actually a vibration of the brake pad against the rotor, which comes out as an audible squeak. The vibration is at a decibel level that sounds like a squeak, so this can occur due to the type of brake pad used or the surface of the rotor.

However, if you have a good brake system and use high quality parts, you should not hear any noise. If noise occurs at some point in the future, you should recognize it as a problem and have the brake system inspected for any wear, tear, or other issue.

Brake Grinding

Grinding usually happens after squeaking. Some brakes never squeak, but go straight to grinding. That is typically metal grinding on metal, and you definitely need to get your vehicle into a shop.

Some of the higher end manufacturers, such as Mercedes, BMW and Lexus, have what are called "brake pad wear indicators." These are just small wires built into the brake pad. Once that wire makes contact with the rotor, a dash light comes on that says "brake wear indicator." At that point, you can bet it is time to replace your pads. Once the sensor makes contact with the rotor, the sensor is ruined and will have to be replaced along with the brake pads.

Squeaky Engine

Many times, you'll find a plastic splash shield installed underneath the front of the car for multiple purposes. These shields not only prevent foreign objects from getting into the engine compartment and causing damage, but also protect against water getting into the drive belt area. If water enters that area, the drive belt may actually slip on the pulleys. You are hearing the squeaking noise because water intrusion has occurred. This is not especially harmful but it probably means that the shield is either disfigured or not there at all.

Shields are frequently damaged when you pull too close to parking spots and hit the sidewalk curb slightly, or when you hit one of those parking stops because your car sits a little bit lower than the average vehicle. If you hit the shield enough times, eventually it will come off.

If that happens, your lower engine area will be exposed and could sustain damage from water, a rock or other debris. Check to see if this plastic shield is in good condition when you wash your car or get fuel. It only takes a moment, and could save you thousands of dollars in repairs.

Thumping While Turning

Sometimes when you turn, you will hear a thumping noise and possibly feel a jerking action through the steering wheel. Several problems could cause this thumping noise.

One problem could be your "constant velocity joints" (or CV joints). Your axle has a constant velocity joint built into it that maintains

40

quickness of motion to the wheels when you turn your steering wheel. When CV joints wear out, they cause a thumping or knocking noise when you turn. The only repair option is to replace the CV joint.

Another thumping noise involves the brakes. Usually occurring at highway speeds, you will hear this when you apply the brakes. It could be something you hear or something you feel. Many times, you see the steering wheel shake.

That usually means the rotors, which are a brake component, are warped. The rotors turn with the wheel as you drive. When you apply the brakes, the brake pads rub against the rotor to create the friction that causes your vehicle to slow down. If the surface of the rotor is not smooth or straight, it produces a thumping noise or a vibration.

Another phrase we hear is described as a "pulsation of the brakes" when they're applied. You typically hear or feel that pulsation when you brake at speeds above 45 miles per hour. You may not necessarily feel the pulsations if you are braking at 20 miles per hour, but once you get up to highway speeds and apply the brakes, you are more likely to feel or hear the vibrations.

Though not necessarily a dangerous situation, it can be quite a nuisance. It also has a negative impact on brake pad and suspension life.

Thumping While Driving

If you hear a regular thumping or vibration that varies with your speed as you're driving down the road, the tires are usually the culprit. Many times, the tread in the tire is separating internally.

Want a sure-fire way to know if this has occurred? Try this: Drive across a parking lot at 2 to 3 miles per hour, then let go of the steering wheel. If your steering wheel shakes back and forth, slightly left to right, that's an indication that the tread has moved inside the tire, and you definitely need to replace the tires.

The age at which you should replace a tire has become an issue over the years. All tires have a number on them that indicates the age of the tire. The number will start with the letters DOT (an abbreviation for Department of Transportation), followed by a series of letters and numbers. At the end of the series will be four digits. Those digits represent the week and year the tire was made. For instance, if one of your tires has the digits 4512, the tire was made in the 45th week of 2012. The numerical significance comes into play because the recommendation for replacing tires is between five and seven years old.

Check your tires. If they are 10 years old, they definitely need to be replaced. If you don't replace them, you are at a great risk of a blow out or tire separation.

Whining Engine

Whining usually occurs either from the children in the back seat or from the car's power steering pump under the hood. You'll want to check both of those possibilities. You may need a cookie for one and power steering fluid for the other.

The power steering fluid is a sealed system for the most part. The fluid does not go away without cause. If you need to add power steering fluid, you most likely have a leak somewhere in the system. Adding fluid will be a temporary measure. If you have a leak, the whine may stop for

42

a while, but once the fluid leaks out again, the whining noise will resume. Take your car for servicing if you suspect a power steering fluid leak.

Vehicle Starting

When you start your car, several noises may be heard. One is a tapping noise that can indicate that your oil is not getting where it needs to be. That noise occurs because some areas of the car need to have oil immediately upon starting. One reason some of the manufacturers have gone to a lighter weight oil is because it can get to those areas that need lubrication quicker on start-up.

Another noise you might hear is a rattling. Any time you hear a rattle in your engine when you start your car, it is metal-to-metal contact. While it will not cause *immediate* failure, problems will happen eventually. The cause is usually a low oil level, low oil pressure, or it could signal that internal wear has occurred.

ENGINE OIL

Here are some common questions about engine oil:

- *Does the type of engine oil I put in really matter?*

- *Can I change the brand of oil I use?*

- *What do the numbers mean?*

All oil today is called "paraffin-based oil." That means the oil has the ability to capture dirt—this is one of its

43

jobs. When an oil change is performed, we drain the oil from the vehicle and dirt goes with it.

Manufacturers have made changes to the oil for use in lubricating their specific engines. The car industry used to recommend oil based on geographic conditions. If you lived in a cold climate, like Alaska, thinner winter oil was recommended. If you lived in the warmer southern states, heavier oil might be recommended.

All that has changed due to the tolerances built into cars by the manufacturers. Today it is more important than ever that you pay attention to the type of oil the manufacturer recommends.

The label on a bottle of oil provides information about that oil. Most people examine the weight of the oil first. Is it 5W-30? 10W-30? What does that even mean? Well, the "W" stands for winter. If we used 5W-30 for example, the "5" and "30" actually measure the thickness, or viscosity, of the oil at different temperatures.

If an oil bottle has "5W30" on it, the oil will have a viscosity of a "5" weight oil when cold and a viscosity of a "30" weight oil when hot. This combination provides an oil that flows well at low temperatures, but still protects the engine at high temperatures. For comparison's sake, SAE 5W-30 and SAE 0W-30 will flow better at even lower temperatures than 10W-30, while still providing protection at high temperatures. Just remember, the "W" stands for winter.[ii]

Most cars today use either 5W-20 or 5W-30, regardless of geographic location. The brand you choose is up to you. Contrary to what your grandfather told you, it's okay to switch brands.

Oil Change Frequency

How often you should change your oil is becoming an issue in our industry because of changes in service intervals. Years ago, it was every three months or three thousand miles. Our fathers, grandfathers and great-grandfathers all taught us that. The reason the oil needed changing so often was because the engines were exposed to the elements, and the filtering system of air and fuel was not what it is today. Your oil could be easily contaminated and cause internal engine damage. That is why car engines used to last only about fifty thousand miles.

Several things have changed since then. With the advent of electronic fuel injection, we do not have as much problem with outside elements getting to the crankcase because the fuel systems are sealed. Fuel is also managed better so the oil is not contaminated with fuel the way it used to be.

Thus, we have better control of outside elements, like dirt and dust, coming into the engine, and we have better control through better filtering. We have better control of the amount of fuel that is dumped into an engine for burning—almost all of it is being burned these days. And finally, the oil has gotten better at suspending the dirt in the engine. When you put these factors together, your service interval can now be longer than it used to be. Some manufacturers will tell you 7,500 miles, some 10,000 miles, and some 15,000 miles. To help simplify things, many cars today have oil life monitors that tell you when it is time to change your oil. My personal opinion is that your oil should be changed every 5,000 miles.

Why do it at 5,000 miles? One reason is because that is the interval at which several other aspects of the car need to be inspected. For example, the tires should be rotated every 5,000 miles. The car ought to be inspected by an ASE Certified Technician at that interval to make sure everything else is working safely and properly.

Some manufacturers have made longer recommendations for oil changes, only to find out that the extended duration between changes caused internal engine damage or failure for the consumer after seventy, eighty or ninety thousand miles. They realized too late that a shorter interval would have extended the car's lifespan.

CHAPTER

6

CAR CARE 201

In this section, let's explore some of the more advanced areas of your vehicle, including when to buy a new one. This could become a reference manual for you and a great training manual for new drivers in your family. I've structured this section in the form of a Question and Answer series, much like the FAQ section of a website or resource book.

SHOULD YOU BUY A NEW CAR?

Let's discuss a few of the most frequently asked questions related to purchasing a new vehicle. Having this information could save you thousands of dollars.

Q. When do I need to buy a new car versus investing in the one I have?

A. Every car has a point of diminishing returns. What you do from the day you drive your car off the showroom floor and whether you think of your vehicle as an investment or as an expense affects the decisions you make about replacing it.

You should not say, "Well, I don't want to put that much money into my car." If you've maintained the car well, you should expect to get 200,000 to 400,000 miles from it. When you buy a vehicle, you have to understand that how you maintain it today is going to determine its condition tomorrow. With proper servicing, your point of diminishing returns is going to be a lot farther down the road than if you neglect it.

I have seen vehicles with as few as 75,000 miles need an engine (between $5,000 and $10,000) simply because the oil was not changed properly.

It is always better to maintain a car correctly from the beginning so that the point of diminishing returns is much farther out than it otherwise would be.

Let's say you have a six or seven-year-old vehicle. Perhaps it needs a timing belt, or has blown a head gasket. It is going to cost $1,500 to $2,500 to repair a vehicle you have been driving for six to seven years. You are just not sure you want to pay that much to get it fixed, so you consider buying a new car. Here's a calculation that may help you decide.

Larry Burkett was a well-known financial advisor who started Crown Financial Ministries. He would tell you that the cheapest car you will ever own is the one in your driveway. What he means is that by having the car maintained and having everything in good working order, you will spend less money than purchasing a newer vehicle.

When we talk about making a major repair on a car, a way you can try to crunch the numbers is to ask yourself, "What's it going to cost me over the next year?" Let's say there is $3,000 worth of work that needs to be done on your vehicle and you have decided you are not going to repair it. Instead, you are going to go buy a used vehicle.

Even if you bought an inexpensive one, around $10,000, there's still the down payment, then the calculated monthly payments if you finance. Of course, depending on the state, you might also have to pay sales tax on that vehicle. In Arizona, you will pay sales tax if you buy from a used car dealer. The vehicle licensing tax will typically increase due to the car being of higher value. Plus, you'll need to figure an almost immediate depreciation, as well. Your insurance will increase because, if you finance the car, you'll have to have full coverage insurance, not to mention it is typically more valuable than the one you are replacing. Calculate your total cost over the next 12 months for that used car and compare that to the cost of making repairs on the one in your driveway.

If you apply this same principle to buying a brand new car, these dollar figures are going to go up exponentially. Therefore, it almost always makes more sense to fix your existing car than to buy a new one.

EXTENDED WARRANTIES

Q: If I buy a new vehicle, should I purchase an extended warranty?

A: I advise my customers against purchasing extended warranties. Evidence proves that, in most cases, the cost of the warranty is far more than the benefit received. The concept I operate under is very simple. An aftermarket warranty company has to make a profit or it goes out of business. It must have significant overhead, with a building and employees and field agents to go out and check a vehicle's needs. For example, if a shop calls and says, this vehicle needs a new transmission, they send an inspector out to make sure that the stated need is valid.

With this huge overhead and the need to make a profit, that almost certainly means that as a group, the people who buy aftermarket warranties are paying far more than the actual cost of repairing their vehicles. Maybe a few people win but most people lose.

We recommend you take the money for the warranty product they're trying to sell you, put it in the bank where it's earning (a little) interest and use it to do routine maintenance on your car.

There are two catches with the warranty policies. First, they may sound like they cover everything but many routine failures aren't covered. Second, nothing is covered *if you haven't had the factory recommended maintenance performed.*

So here's the trick. If you do the factory recommended maintenance, the chances of having a breakdown on those covered components are very slim. You don't *need* an extended warranty because you know maintenance pays off. You win by keeping your money and investing it in maintenance rather than purchasing an extended warranty and hoping that if anything goes wrong, it will be something that's covered.

If, after reading this book, you decide to purchase an extended warranty, please—do *not* include it in the financing of your car. It truly is not a good investment, and paying interest on it only makes it worse.

Note: If you're interested in learning more about this topic, see *Appendix I* in the back of this book.

CARING FOR YOUR CAR

Q. When should I jump-start my car?

A. The primary purpose of a battery is to send power to the starter, which then starts the engine. If a problem with the battery exists, it will show up when you try to start the car, not while you're driving.

We've all experienced a dead battery, haven't we? We turn the key and either hear nothing or series of repetitive clicks. The

51

engine does not turn over. That is the only time you should jump-start your car.

If you're driving down the road and your car dies, the battery is not the cause of your car dying. Do not jump-start your car in this situation. It will not help.

Note: See the "*How-To*" Section to learn the proper way to jump-start your car.

PREMIUM FUEL

Q. Do I need to buy premium fuel?

A. The best way to determine if premium fuel is right for you is to check your owner's manual to see what they recommend for your specific car. Higher-end models may require premium gas. Those cars are designed to burn fuel at optimum levels. Both the way the engine is timed and tuned, and the type of spark plugs used ensures that when you use this fuel, you'll get the optimum performance from your vehicle.

There is nothing wrong with using fuel rated at 87 octane if a higher-octane fuel is not advised by the manufacturer. Components called "knock sensors" were added to vehicles a few years ago. These sensors adjust the timing if the engine begins to "ping" or "knock" due to lower octane or other factors in the fuel.

So do you have to use premium fuel? The answer is no. However, if you want the best performance and the best fuel mileage for your particular vehicle, then I recommend using higher quality gasoline, usually only available at nationally branded fuel stations, not discount fuel stations.

The return on investment is simply a crunching of the numbers. (Keep in mind that other factors affect gas mileage, as well—how fast we drive, driving conditions, environmental factors, and more.)

If you want to keep your vehicle in the best running condition and keep your fuel economy at its best, it is worth the small price to use high quality fuels. These fuels contain important additives, such as cleaners, that discount fuels do not have. I personally use and recommend Chevron fuel due to their patented "Techron" cleaning agent although any top-tier brand of fuel is preferable to "discount" fuels. Occasional use of "discount" fuels is fine since frequent use of high quality fuels will still keep the fuel injectors clean and operating efficiently.

MOTOR CLUB MEMBERSHIPS

Q. How beneficial are motor club memberships?

A. Motor clubs provide good benefits for the consumer and offer peace of mind for the consumer who travels a lot or has a loved one living away from home. Undoubtedly, their primary focus is the customer. I am thinking of clubs like AAA Motor Club or Cross Country Motor Club, the two big wheels in the industry.

It's easy to feel vulnerable when traveling through an unfamiliar part of the country. These clubs help locate a reliable repair facility, a towing company, a hotel, and other things of that nature. Therefore, you have more confidence in the quality of service you will receive.

CHAPTER

7

INTRODUCTION TO MAINTENANCE

What do we mean when we say, "maintenance?" It's a term that applies to any number of industries and essentially means the same thing in each—it means *care* or *upkeep*.

We've already discussed crucial factors in the care and upkeep of your vehicle—things like engine oils, the benefits of regular services, and so on. Let's address a few other important components of your car's maintenance.

VEHICLE FLUIDS

Transmission Fluid

In the section on motor oil, we covered the fact that dirt is suspended in the oil. At each oil change, the oil (and the dirt it holds) drains out of your car and clean oil is added. Can we apply the same reasoning with transmissions?

Transmissions don't pull in air, but they do have metal-to-metal contact, or the potential for metal-to-metal contact (this is true with every component on your car where fluids are involved). Transmissions also produce great amounts of heat.

Heat, plus metal-to-metal contact eventually breaks down the fluid that circulates through the system. The good news is that we do not have to service the transmission every 5,000 miles. Most experts advise servicing the transmission every 30,000 miles, especially if your vehicle is used for towing (boats, campers, etc.). If you're not towing and don't do a lot of driving, then you could probably extend your regular transmission service to 50,000 miles. Typically, the manufacturer has a recommendation as well. Check with your owner's manual.

Differential Fluid

We can apply this same concept to the differential. On most front-wheel-drive vehicles, the differential is a part of the transmission. The differential on rear-wheel-drive cars is located in the rear axle. Differentials also need occasional fluid changes. The proper interval is usually described in your owner's manual.

Power Steering Fluid

These same principles and guidelines apply to the power steering system. This system is predominantly a "closed" or "sealed" system, but over time, this fluid needs to be changed to protect the components from wearing from the inside. Remember, it is always less expensive to change the fluid that protects the part than to replace the part itself.

Brake Fluid

Unlike the previous aspects of maintenance, brake fluid is not added at particular intervals. Instead, we can measure when brake fluid or coolant should be changed. The measurement for when brake fluid should be flushed is 200 copper parts per million.

Brake fluid is hygroscopic, which means that if you left the can open overnight, the contents would be ruined because the moisture it would absorb overnight would render it unusable inside your vehicle. It is *imperative* to keep brake fluid tightly sealed.

Brake fluid is designed to absorb moisture in your brake system since moisture deteriorates all the metal components the brake fluid comes in contact with. Brake fluid is a hydraulic fluid crucial to proper braking.

If your brake fluid becomes too heated (especially if it heats to boiling) it creates air bubbles. If you've ever had air in your system, you know that the brake pedal goes to the floor and still doesn't stop the car! It's a horrifying experience. Moisture contamination over time greatly reduces the temperature at which brake fluid will form vapor (air bubbles) due to heat. The moisture also causes the fluid to become corrosive to all of the metal parts in the system.

Once the fluid reaches 200 copper parts per million due to normal wear in the system components, the brake fluid's corrosion influence is greatly increased, which could potentially cause problems. The destruction to your brakes would not occur suddenly, so by the time it causes actual problems, your system could already be ruined—which will be quite an expensive repair.

Since we have started doing brake flushes on vehicles, we seldom have to replace the calipers. Some companies will recommend putting new calipers on your car as part of a routine brake job, but typically, they are not needed.

Most brake flushes currently cost less than $150, and need to be done every two to four years (depending on fluid measurements and the environment), whereas brake caliper replacements will often cost between $300 and $600. Luckily, in the desert southwest, moisture contamination is not as common as elsewhere in the country.

That's another important reason you should take your car to a licensed technician who will keep it in proper running condition and replace fluids appropriately. The old Ben Franklin quote about an ounce of prevention being worth a pound of cure is really true when it comes to maintenance on your car.

Cooling System Fluid: Antifreeze/Coolant

The cooling system's primary component is antifreeze/coolant, which helps keep the engine from freezing in the winter (don't laugh, we do travel to other climates you know), and keeps it cool in the summer. As with brake fluid, your coolant can be tested to determine when it needs to be replaced.

In this case, we measure the pH level, which is an indicator of the acidic protection that the fluid is capable of providing, and the freeze point. For instance, a pH level of 7.0 is neutral, indicating that the coolant is no longer protecting the soft metals inside your engine. It's like having straight water in your cooling system, which is detrimental because it deteriorates the metal inside the system. This shortens the life of your heater core, radiator, intake manifolds and cylinder heads.

The cooling system should be checked regularly, usually during routine oil changes. Many cooling system repairs will cost $500 to $1,000. In contrast, having the cooling system flushed costs less than $150 for most vehicles. You save long-term dollars by maintaining your vehicle on a regular basis.

Air Conditioning System Fluids/Refrigerant

In states with sweltering, hot summers, few things are more frustrating than having your air conditioning blow hot air when it is over 100° outside. Proper maintenance can prevent this.

Your air conditioning system is a sealed system. We know from previous discussions in closed systems, the only way you lose fluid, or in this case refrigerant, is when you have a leak in the system. Having the air conditioning evaluated and recharged about every three to five years is a good maintenance guideline, even if it seems to be working well.

The A/C system is critically dependent on oil carried throughout the system by the refrigerant. If you have a leak in the system, the oil may not circulate properly to protect those expensive A/C components. Just like running your engine without oil, running your A/C system without proper oiling will damage your A/C "engine," (also known as the compressor).

Some compressors look like very small engines on the inside. They have some of the same components as your car's engine—pistons, rings, rods and a crankshaft—only much smaller. Keeping the compressor well lubricated extends its longevity.

59

You should *always* have your A/C system serviced by an ASE Certified Technician. It's just too risky to do it yourself. Keeping your air conditioning system serviced when necessary is a great way to save money and stay cool in the heat of summer.

> *NEVER* attempt to recharge your air conditioning system yourself!

TESTING AND DIAGNOSIS

Years ago, a technician might spend five minutes diagnosing a car and five hours making the repair. Today, we might spend five hours running tests and diagnosing the vehicle, and five minutes repairing or putting a component on it. The use of electronics drives this change.

Vehicles today have a tremendous number of electronic systems. It is not unusual to find between five and fifteen computers on any given car. It is imperative that all those computers communicate with each other. The main computer is the Powertrain Control Module. All other computers must communicate with this "mission control center" through a CAN—Controller Area Network. Investigating these various computer systems can become complex.

Again, this is where experienced, certified technicians are worth their weight in gold. Let the professionals do their jobs—taking care of the upkeep for your car.

60

CHAPTER

8

CAR CARE 301

No book like this would be complete without a "How To" section. There are many things on a car that you can do yourself, and in this section, I want to discuss the proper way to do them.

YOUR AUTOMOTIVE "HOW TO" GUIDE

How to Change a Flat Tire

Most modern vehicles have a tire pressure monitoring system that will indicate that you have a low tire. Technology has improved to the point that some cars even tell you which tire is low, so pay attention to your dash lights. If that light comes on, you need to quickly find a safe place to investigate the situation.

Tires can go flat over a short *or* a long period, depending on the size of the leak. When you need to change a tire, the most dangerous place for you to change it is on the edge of the interstate highway. If possible, get off the highway, even if that means driving on the shoulder at a very slow speed until you can exit—or at least to an area of the road where you can safely pull off the road (which to me is at least 10 to 15 feet from the edge of the highway). Ideally, you want to exit and get to a safe location out of sight of the highway, where you can raise the car using the tools provided. A lighted area is preferable if this happens at night.

If you've never changed a flat before, let me encourage you to practice doing so in the safety and comfort of your garage or driveway. Become familiar with the tools and the procedure. Follow the directions given in the driver's manual. If you have children of or near driving age, demonstrate the technique to them and then let them duplicate the process. The last thing you want to do is figure out how to change a flat when you're pulled off the side of a road!

The owner's manual will tell you the exact location where you must place the jack in order to raise the vehicle safely. You can damage your car, or injure yourself, if you place it incorrectly. Here's another little hint: Always loosen (but don't remove) the lug nuts holding the wheel in

62

place *before* you jack up the car. It's much easier to remove the tire if you do it that way.

When putting the spare tire on, be sure to start each of the lug nuts by hand. Remember to put the beveled edge of the lug nut toward the wheel. Then, with your tire iron, tighten them in a star pattern. To do this, tighten one, then skip one, tighten one, then skip one. Eventually, all five nuts will be tight.

> **Note:** Tighten the lug nuts as best you can with the wheel off the ground. Then you can lower the jack completely and re-tighten in the star pattern with the wheel firmly on the ground.

Most cars come with the wrench or tire iron you use to tighten the lug nuts. To make it easier to change the tire, position the wrench in such a way that you can stand on it, using your leg and body weight to loosen each lug nut. However, you do not want to do that while tightening the lug nuts (because you can over-tighten them). After tightening all of the lug nuts, drive 50 to 100 miles, and then check them again to make sure they are still tight.

HOW TO JUMP-START A CAR

Jump-starting a car is actually applying a boost of electricity. You're running an electrical current from one battery to another. That gives you two batteries with the potential to ignite vented acid gas you know as hydrogen. Therefore, a carefully controlled boost of electricity reduces the risk of injury and/or damage.

63

What we mean by "venting" is that it's not uncommon for battery fumes from the acid inside to slowly leak from the top of the battery. Since hydrogen is explosive, you could potentially blow up the battery if you don't control that spark. And, if your face happens to be in the vicinity at the time, bad things could happen. If you have safety glasses, it would be a good idea to wear them when you jump-start a car.

Here's how to properly jump-start a car:

Note: The car with the "good" battery should *not* be running at this point.

1. Connect the red jumper cable clamp to the positive terminal (+) of the "good" battery.
2. Connect the other end of that red cable to the positive terminal of the "bad" battery.
3. Connect the black cable clamp to the negative (-) terminal of the "good" battery.
4. Connect the final cable clamp to a good solid metal surface under the hood of the car being "jumped," such as a bracket or other metal object. If necessary, you can attach to the negative terminal of the battery, it's just not as safe.
5. Now have the driver of the "good" car start the engine and run it at just above idle for a couple of minutes.
6. Then, attempt to start the car with the dead battery. If done correctly and the problem is just a dead battery, the car should start right up.
7. Carefully remove the cables in reverse order.

Jump-starting a car essentially uses electricity from the good battery to power the bad one, thus making an electrical circuit. Making the last connection to the engine instead of the battery will minimize the possibility of an uncontrolled spark, thus keeping you and your battery safe.

Jump Starting a Car: Illustration

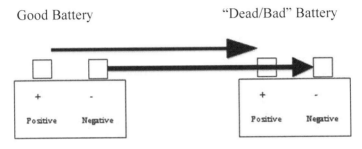

Good Battery   "Dead/Bad" Battery

Connect Positive to Positive

THEN

Connect Negative to Negative
(or to solid metal surface)

When jump-starting a car, remember:

+ to + THEN − to −

How to Manage a Breakdown

You should be familiar enough with your gauges to know what "normal" is, so when the gauges are not within normal range, you will realize something is wrong.

When you are driving, and begin to feel something about the function of your car that you are unsure about, or hear a new noise,

65

cautiously move into the right lane. You do *not* want your vehicle to be disabled in the left lane or in the median of a freeway. Always try to get to a safe location to manage a breakdown.

If your vehicle begins to overheat, the gauges will indicate it, so keep an eye on them. If your vehicle *is* overheating, turn the engine off as soon as possible.

The second thing you should do during a breakdown is to make a call. These days most people carry cell phones. I recommend you keep numbers for a towing company, motor club or repair shop in your phone for such an emergency. You can call us at 928-783-9309 for 24-hour towing service and we'll get help to you right away.

Make sure you're in a safe spot and keep passengers a safe distance from the highway while you wait for help to arrive. This will decrease your risk of an accident. Managing a breakdown, though sometimes nerve-racking and always inconvenient, is not that complicated. Try to remember the following:

1. Don't panic!
2. Think "safety."
3. Call for assistance.

HOW TO MANAGE AN ACCIDENT

Having an accident is always an emotional situation—whether that emotion is anger, frustration, fear, sorrow, anxiety, worry or panic. Even something as minor as a fender-bender or a slow-speed parking lot accident can be enough to create emotion. Try to remain calm.

When you are in an accident, remember first that insurance companies typically investigate accidents to determine fault—so don't assume or admit that you are the guilty party. Being in an emotional state or in a state of shock can skew your perception of the accident. Let them do their job.

Next, call the police. Once they are on their way, exchange insurance information with the other driver. You probably don't need to worry about writing any information down—just use your cell phone to take pictures of their driver's license, their car, them, and the area. Make sure you get proof of insurance from the other driver. If they have the necessary information available at the scene, call immediately to verify that they do have coverage. Just because the paper says they are covered doesn't mean they are. You should always have your insurance information in the glove compartment to give the other party.

For most states, unless there's bodily injury, you should remove the vehicle from the road. You can be cited for obstruction of traffic if you keep your car on the road when there's no personal injury. Remove your car to a safe place and proceed to work out the details with the other party as you await the arrival of the police.

Tow trucks dispatched by the police are often under contract with the police. Typically, they will tow your vehicle to their lot and charge you storage fees while it's there. These fees can mount up quickly, especially if there is a dispute with your insurance company regarding your claim and your vehicle can't be repaired right away.

You have the option of having your vehicle towed to a collision repair facility of your choosing. Most collision repair facilities allow cars to remain there, free of charge, while the insurance company details are resolved. This can save you a significant amount of money in storage fees.

It's a good idea to think ahead and be prepared. Know where you want your car taken if you should have an accident. If your car care shop doesn't do body work, ask them to recommend someone you can trust, and keep their phone number and address in your glove box, along with your insurance information.

HOW TO MANAGE BEING STUCK IN TRAFFIC

The one thing you want to avoid is becoming trapped behind the car in front of you. The way I avoid that is to stop far enough behind that I can still see their rear tires touching the pavement. That way, I can maneuver around it if I need to.

You've heard of, or perhaps have been a part of, a pile up where one car rams into the car in front of them and it causes a domino effect. If you leave enough space between you and the car in front of you, you're not trapped; you can swing your car to either side and avoid being rammed from behind.

Sometimes traffic jams simply cannot be avoided. That's another reason to keep more than a quarter tank of gas in your car. You don't want to run out at a time like that.

Always watch your temperature gauge when you're stopped in traffic. Most cars are designed to be able to idle indefinitely—even with the air conditioning on. Still, you need to watch that gauge. If you notice your engine heating up, roll your windows down and turn off the air conditioning.

Traffic jams happen in the winter, as well. Some states require you to have a safety kit in your vehicle. The kit usually contains items like bottled water, a blanket and a flashlight. It's not a bad idea. You never know when you'll be caught in traffic, or how long it will take to clear the roads.

DRIVING IN SEVERE CONDITIONS

How to Drive in Sandstorms

Here in the desert southwest, sandstorms can be extremely dangerous, often sending visibility to near zero. If you are caught in a sandstorm, as visibility diminishes, so should your speed.

Your safest option is to exit a freeway or busy street and find a safe place to park such as a shopping mall or other commercial area, before visibility is severely reduced, and simply wait out the storm. If that isn't possible, and visibility becomes nearly zero, you need to pull off the road. Once you pull off the road, don't make the potentially fatal mistake of keeping your foot on the brake or turning on your emergency flashers. Making yourself visible is precisely what you should *not* do.

When you're caught in a sand storm, pull as far off the roadway on the right side as it is safely possible to do. If you can get completely off the shoulder, off the paved surface, and do so safely, you want to do that. Then you want to extinguish all lighting, make sure your foot is not on the brake, turn your headlights off and do not turn on your emergency flashers.

You may be thinking, "Is this guy nuts? If I turn all my lights off, someone's likely to run into me!"

Studies have shown the opposite is true. In poor visibility situations, other drivers will track right in on your lights, assume you're moving and smash into your stationary vehicle. Maybe they think that you can magically see through the sand when they can't, so they're going to follow you. I'm sure you've heard of accidents like this. Because of this phenomenon, you want to extinguish all your lighting when you pull over and stop.

How to Drive in Desert Southwest Thunderstorms

Thunderstorms are another danger in our part of the country, often coming hard on the heels of dust storms. The desert sand doesn't soak up much water, so our dry washes suddenly fill with fast moving, deep water. It creates a very dangerous situation, especially when the thunderstorm occurs miles away and the wash fills with no warning. (For newcomers, a "wash" is created by rainwater running off the desert sand in sheets, gathering in low spots and carving out these miniature "canyons" that range from three to over fifteen feet deep.)

In 2012, four people in Arizona lost their lives in flash floods.[iii] Half of all fatalities in flash floods are people who attempted to drive through flooded washes. Numerous people are injured when they try to drive through a wash with swift-moving water. Even if they're not injured, they may lose their vehicles.

The owners of huge SUVs or pickups, and we have quite a few of those around here, frequently attempt to drive through running washes. I don't advise it. Don't assume, if they're successful, that you can follow them in your Prius. Everyone should think safety first. That wash will probably be empty, or the flow will be greatly diminished, within thirty minutes to an hour. Taking a chance and trying to drive through it, just to save thirty minutes, is simply not worth the risk.

How to Drive on Snow and Ice

Snow and ice certainly provide challenges to drivers. (Don't laugh; you may travel to snowy or icy conditions.) When driving on snow you need increased traction. That's why four-wheel-drive vehicles (or front-wheel-drive vehicles) get around better—simply because of their superior traction.

In deep snow, one tip that might come in handy is to lower the air pressure in your tires to about 25 pounds of pressure. You still won't be able to drive fast, but since there's more rubber on the road, you'll notice an improvement in your ability to negotiate snowy road conditions. Note: It is important to remember to drive slowly, never at high speeds until you re-inflate the tires. Once you get to plowed roads you will need to inflate the tires to the specified pressure right away.

We learned years ago to gently pump the brakes in the snow, but the best advice I can offer is to drive as though you had an egg under the gas and brake pedals. Accelerate slowly and brake gently. Don't push on the pedals too strongly. You'll break the eggs!

HOW TO BUY A USED CAR

Buying a used car can be risky business. Let me offer some strategies that might prove helpful in that situation.

First, do your homework. Look online, read consumer magazines, peruse some used car lots, investigate the "For Sale" ads in your newspaper and check out *Kelley Blue Book* for reasonable pricing. Take all the time you need to figure out exactly what you're interested in—make, model and even options.

Once you've narrowed your search, it's time to find that perfect vehicle—whether you intend to buy from an individual or a car dealership. Study the car, walk around it and look at it from different angles. Once you finish assessing the cosmetic aspects, then sit behind the steering wheel. Touch everything you can touch. Check out the wipers, the radio, the heat and air, the glove box and the lights. Make sure everything works, including turn signals, power windows, power locks, power seats, rear wipers, and so on.

If everything checks out, let the seller know you'd like to take about 45 minutes to an hour to road test this car. If they want to ride with you, that's fine, but make sure they're willing for you to spend the time you need.

Most people drive the car around the block or spend ten minutes driving up the road and back and say, "I'll take it"—but not you. You're too savvy for that. During your test drive, listen to the vehicle. Notice the way it feels, handles and steers. You don't have to be an automotive mechanic to know if something is not quite right.

If you hear a noise that concerns you, or there's a shake or shimmy in the steering, or anything else that doesn't quite seem right, then make note of it. Spend time driving both on the freeway at highway speeds and in town at normal speeds. See how the vehicle take corners, slows, stops, accelerates—just as you would drive the vehicle on any given day.

Use your senses. Don't play the radio. Make sure the radio plays, then turn it off and listen. Use your five senses to note if anything seems abnormal.

If everything checks out, move to the next step—take it to an ASE-certified technician for a used-car inspection. If you bring it to us, we'll check it out for a small fee. Our trained technician will inspect the exterior and interior of the car, take it for a drive, bring it back into the bay and raise it up to do a more thorough inspection. The technician will know exactly the kinds of things to look for, the kinds of things that could signal a future problem.

Please, don't wait until you've already bought it! One of the worst things we experience is when one of our clients comes in and says, "Hey, can you check this car out for me? I just bought it. Just check it over and let me know what it needs."

We always cringe when we hear they've already bought it. Checking it out has led to people actually standing there in our shop and

73

crying. We've found cars that have been badly wrecked and just repaired enough to look good cosmetically, not repaired structurally. In addition, we often find other major mechanical problems and frequently find there has been a severe lack of routine maintenance, which can spell major problems ahead. Never buy a used vehicle until after the shop you trust has checked it out for you. We understand how devastating it can be to learn, after the fact, that someone has sold you *their* problem.

If the person you are buying from does not want to allow you to take the car to a shop, then walk away. There's a reason for it. Don't bring us every car that you look at, just bring us the car you think that you have your heart set on. Our charge is minimal and in fact, if we see there's major damage, we won't even charge you for it, we just tell you to run away from this and bring us another one.

The inspection fee is a very small investment for having us look the vehicle over, finding out what the maintenance and/or repair needs are and giving you an itemized list with prices. Now you have something to take back to the seller as a bargaining chip.

You can take that list back to the owner and say, "I had the vehicle checked out, here's the list of things it needs. If you knock off half (or whatever) of the cost on this list, I'll buy the car."

You can use that list to get a better deal on the vehicle and then apply that money toward the maintenance items. Once you get that list, always include those costs in the purchase price when you're thinking about what you're paying for the vehicle. For example, if your price limit is $4,000 and we find $1,500 worth of maintenance needs on a car priced at $3,500, you need to think twice. You would be spending $5,000 on this car to bring all of the maintenance up to snuff and have a good solid starting point. So you're now $1,000 over your limit. Is that vehicle really worth it?

The ASE-certified technician can help you decide about repairs that need to be done now or in the near future as opposed to those that can be deferred. That will also give you greater wisdom and leverage in making an offer to the seller. Once you decide to buy this particular car, you're ready for the final step—making the deal.

You should not talk about price, or make any offer until you have taken all these steps. Then you'll be able to approach the seller and tell them, "I'd like to buy this car. I've had it inspected and here is the estimate of the items that need attention to get it into satisfactory condition. With that in mind, I'm willing to pay this amount for it—and if that's agreeable with you, I'm ready to buy it today."

Of course, we may find the vehicle you're considering is in great shape. And when you get an "all clear" from someone who truly knows what they're doing, it will give you great confidence. But if that's not the case, you are now in a better position to make a good deal.

That is the right way to buy a vehicle. Constrain your emotions, have a certified technician inspect it and know what you are getting into before you make an offer. By following this process, you will save yourself from some unpleasant surprises that could cost you a lot of money.

CHAPTER

9

FINDING A GOOD REPAIR SHOP

If you're moving out of your current area, one of the best actions you could take in finding a reliable repair shop is to ask your current one. Most shops are in some kind of network or association and they may know a good shop in the area where you're relocating.

If you're looking to find a reliable repair shop in your current locale, here are some tips about finding one you'll be happy with. Do some investigation. First, ask others if they're satisfied with their shops. If you ask ten people and three or four of them give you the same name, you're probably on to something.

Additionally, find out if the shop is affiliated with any associations. I have yet to meet somebody who is a member of ASA and/or is affiliated with AAA, who doesn't run an excellent company. When shop owners understand the value of affiliating with a national organization and affiliating with other shop owners for the good of the industry, you can be reassured that they run a good shop.

You should check to see if they are an accredited member of the Better Business Bureau. All small business owners should understand the value of that association. Then check with your local Better Business Bureau to see what their rating is and whether they've had any complaints that haven't been resolved.

When you've narrowed down your choices, move to the next step. Call the shop and ask some questions.

> **Note:** See the next section for a summary of these questions
> and others you should ask when making your calls**.**

Find out whether their technicians are ASE certified and if they are required to participate in continuing education/training. Ascertain to what extent they service your particular make and model. Do they have the software to communicate with the computer systems on your vehicle? Do they have the specialized tools your car may require?

Ask if they utilize a system of reminders to let you know when it's time for service. Do they have a schedule in place to keep your car well maintained?

Finally, ask a simple question about your vehicle, maybe about their procedure when you have a check engine light on. Just give them an opportunity to speak to you so you can see how they sound. If they sound rushed, as if they don't have time for you, there might be a problem there. If you don't feel comfortable after that conversation, it's probably not going to get any better when they have possession of your vehicle.

If you *do* feel comfortable, you're probably on to a good shop. Then, drive by their location and just look them over. Observe the cars in their parking lot or in the service bays if you can see inside. Do you see a mix of cars similar to yours or those in your neighborhood? Does it look like they work on cars like yours? Does the shop appear to be clean, well lit and well maintained?

Watch for bad signs, like dusty, broken-down looking cars in the parking lot, maybe sitting on a jack stand with the wheel off. Cars that have obviously been sitting in the parking lot for a long time are not a good sign. Something like that should definitely set alarm bells ringing.

Compare the shops you visit. Make an informed decision and choose the one that looks like it will best meet your needs based on these steps.

Then, make an appointment for something relatively simple and easy—preferably an oil change. When you take your car in, speak to the Service Advisor there. You should feel comfortable and confident talking with them. If you don't, you might want to try another shop. You should always be comfortable with the people you are dealing with.

Tell them you'll wait for your car to be ready. While you're waiting, look and listen. You can learn a lot by doing that. Pay attention

79

to how employees interact with each other and with other customers. Notice how they answer the phone. If possible, watch the way they handle your car. It won't take long before you arrive at an opinion about how professionally they run their shop. That can go a long way in helping you make a decision.

When your car is ready, a thorough shop will have information for you because they've conducted a multi-point inspection of your car, regardless of the type of service they performed. They should assure you either that your car is in great shape or provide you with a list of recommended maintenance or repair items.

Ask questions about the recommendations, as many as it takes to feel comfortable with the person you're dealing with or to understand the issue with your vehicle, to understand why they're making those recommendations, and what the benefit is to you for following their advice. If you don't understand what they tell you, ask again. It's the Service Advisor's job to answer your questions fully and to your satisfaction. If you've asked the question twice and they just made you feel stupid, they're not doing a good job. Knowledge is power and they should make you feel empowered.

You should never feel pressured to make a decision about additional services on the spot. You may want to take their recommendations and compare them to the factory-recommended service intervals in your owner's manual. Although those intervals may not match up, the Service Advisor should be able to explain why you might need a particular service earlier than the factory recommendation. If not, you are probably right to be concerned about the shop's ethics.

80

Remember, here in the desert southwest, we fall into the "Severe Conditions" service category in your owner's manual.

By the time you've done all the homework outlined above, you shouldn't have any issues when you take your car in the first time. *But,* if for any reason you are not completely satisfied with your service, give them an opportunity to make it right with you. You can tell a lot about the culture of the business by how they handle a customer concern.

SIX QUESTIONS TO ASK A SHOP

Once you've checked their credentials as thoroughly as possible, call the top shops on your list to narrow down your choices. Following are the six simple questions you can ask any shop. (As a word of caution, let me note that it's extremely dangerous to choose a shop based on their pricing. There's simply too much room for misunderstanding and manipulation if price is your only criteria.) That's why I advise you to ask these six questions and compare the answers you receive:

1. What is your warranty?
2. Are your technicians ASE-Certified and do you have any ASE Master Technicians?
3. Are your technicians required to participate in continuing education/training?
4. Do you provide a free round-trip shuttle or loaner vehicle?
5. Do you have the software and any specialized tools required to work on (my vehicle)?

81

6. Do you have a system that keeps a maintenance schedule for vehicles and notifies me when it's time for service?

These six simple questions will successfully point you to the best shop in your area. But sometimes, even when you've found an excellent shop, things don't always go as expected. I'd like to prepare you for those situations.

DEALING WITH YOUR SHOP

It's very common in this industry for new issues to become apparent only after something is dismantled—things that couldn't have been apparent before the job began. For that reason, upgrading an estimate in the middle of a job is not necessarily a bad thing. However, you certainly have the right to ask questions so you understand why the estimate is changing.

The answers should make sense to you so you feel comfortable. You want to ask the following questions:

- How important is this additional item?

- Is it a safety, reliability or maintenance issue?

- What's the possible impact if I don't do it now?

- Will I save money by having you do this now, "while you're in there," rather than waiting and paying you to dismantle everything to go back and fix it later?

You need the answers to these questions so you can make an informed decision about when and whether to have the additional work done. For example, if the technician found a small leak in your radiator, the coolant level can become too low and it can cost you several thousand dollars due to overheating if not repaired.

Your decision on something like that will be obvious. Other maintenance items won't have a major short-term impact and a good shop will tell you so, allowing you to float the work off for several months. That way, you can schedule it according to your budget.

Any time you're presented with a list of recommendations, ask them to rank them in order of importance. Safety is always first, reliability is always second and standard maintenance items are always third.

The Service Advisor you're working with should be able to easily categorize the work your vehicle needs in that way. He or she should be able to work with you and help you make a plan if you choose to defer some of the work. A good shop will always work with you in a way that benefits you, not them.

When Things Go Wrong

What if you have a problem? What if you feel you haven't been treated fairly or they've blown past the estimate and you weren't informed? Or what if they didn't fix your problem, made it worse or introduced a new one? No business is perfect all the time, and even the best shop makes mistakes occasionally. You need to know the best way to handle those situations.

The first step is to speak to the Service Advisor and give them an opportunity to make it right. Typically, the Service Advisor with a good repair company will work with you and do whatever it takes to make it right. If you're not satisfied with their efforts, call and schedule an appointment with the owner.

Sit down and calmly explain your situation to the owner. It is a very rare owner who does not want to make things right for you. Give them an opportunity. The last thing you want to do is to get angry and take your vehicle somewhere else and pay to have the work done again and then begin litigation to recoup that money. Nobody wins at that game and it's a lengthy, stressful situation.

Obviously, if you're not satisfied after speaking with the owner, litigation may be your only recourse. In my experience though, if you give the owner an opportunity to make it right, they will. But be sure you take the right approach when discussing your problem. No ranting and raving and wild accusations! You don't want to take the offensive—people instinctively want to help *nice* people, not someone who's demanding and angry. (They will help someone with an overbearing attitude, for the sake of the business, but they're more likely to go the extra mile for someone who is being gracious.) Keep calm, stick to the issues and seek a satisfactory resolution.

CHAPTER

IO

CONCLUSION

Thank you so much for reading this book. I hope it is a blessing in your life. It's been a pleasure writing it and I feel good about imparting this knowledge to help you. I hope what you've read will make you feel more empowered when you are dealing with automotive repair issues.

I recommend that you keep a copy in your glove box for future reference. If you've found it helpful, please buy a copy for someone else—your children, friends or other family members—anyone who can benefit from this information.

You can buy this book from Amazon or at Accurate Automotive Attention. If something you've read sparks a question or makes you think, *Wow! I need to have* that *done,* you can visit our website, www.YumaCarCare.com, for additional information or to make an appointment. Or, please call us:

Central location:	928.783.8808
Yuma Foothills:	928.342.1912
Express Auto/RV (Foothills):	928.305.0767

Please don't hesitate to call me. I'll be happy to spend all the time with you that you need and answer any questions you might have.

Again, thank you for reading my book. I look forward to seeing or meeting you and signing your copy!

I

APPENDIX I: EXTENDED WARRANTIES

First, extended warranties are all over the board. A dealership typically offers two types. One is the type the manufacturer offers, so if I bought a Subaru, it would be a Subaru extended warranty. If I bought a GM, it would be a GM extended warranty. The dealership also offers an "after-market extended warranty." That is usually serviced by a company whose sole product is extended warranties.

For whatever reason, most after-market extended warranty companies are located or originated in the St. Louis area. The St. Louis Better Business Bureau and the St. Louis Attorney General spend significant time dealing with these companies because of consumer complaints.

ConsumerAffairs.com says, "From what we've heard, we suspect that most extended warranties are a waste of money that could be better spent on performing exquisite maintenance, still the best insurance of trouble-free motoring." They also said, "Sixty-five percent (or more than 8,000) *Consumer Reports* readers surveyed by the Consumer Reports National Research Center in the winter of 2011 said they spent significantly more for a new car warranty than they got back in repair cost savings." That is very common.

(*http://www.consumeraffairs.com/news04/2005/extended_warranty.html*)

There are even conventions for these companies that teach how to sell an extended warranty. The following quotation is from the website, *WarrantyInnovations.com*. It explains the whole purpose of the convention, throughout all their breakout sessions and their main course.

"The discussion will also include ways to leverage systems and data to drive extended warranty sales, how to build a recurring revenue stream with extended warranties in maintenance, *lower costs, and claims* against your program and how to better work with your insurance and our administrator."

That information clearly states that their intent is *to sell more warranties and reduce the number of claims*. Extended warranties are a contract, and I learned a long time ago that contracts are usually written in favor of those who write them.

Without question, extended warranty contracts are not good for the consumer. Can you find people who have been able to save money in buying an extended warranty? Yes, you can. The response rate, according to *Consumer Reports*, is about one in five—so about 20% said they had a net savings.

The *Consumer Reports* study basically says that when you're buying a car, it is better *not* to buy an extended warranty, but instead use those dollars to maintain your vehicle. In the survey, respondents cited warranty costs of $1,000 on average that provided benefits of $700—a $300 loss. Forty-two percent of extended warranties were never used, and only about a third of all respondents used their plan to cover a serious problem.

There are also exclusions from coverage by an extended warranty. So, even though you purchased the warranty, you're still going to have to pay for repairs that are not covered. Beware, because there is a lot of fine print in those contracts. Read it carefully if you're considering purchasing a warranty.

<u>Most extended warranties give the warranty company the option of putting used parts on your car</u>. So if your transmission goes out, instead of getting a new transmission, you could get a used one—one out of a salvage yard or from a recycler. It's their choice, not yours. That's scary, but it saves them money.

All in all, it's really pretty simple. The warranty companies have to make a profit to stay in business, they have considerable overhead such as personnel, buildings, office infrastructure, advertising, etc. This requires that overall they take in far more money than they spend on repairs. As a total group, the consumer loses. They have to, or the company would fail.

II

APPENDIX II: ASA CODE OF ETHICS

To perform high quality repair service at a fair and just price.

To use only proven merchandise of high quality distributed by reputable firms.

To employ the best skilled technicians obtainable.

To furnish an itemized invoice for fairly priced parts and services that clearly identifies any used or remanufactured parts. Replaced parts may be inspected upon request.

To have a sense of personal obligation to each customer.

To promote good will between the motorist and members of the association.

To recommend corrective and maintenance services, explaining to the customer which of these are required to correct existing problems and which are for preventive maintenance.

To offer the customer a price estimate for work to be performed.

To furnish or post copies of any warranties covering parts or services.

To obtain prior authorization for all work done, in writing, or by other means satisfactory to the customer.

To notify the customer if appointments or completion promises cannot be kept.

To maintain customer service records for one year or more.

To exercise reasonable care for the customer's property while in our possession.

To maintain a system for fair settlement of customer's complaints.

To cooperate with established consumer complaint mediation activities.

To uphold the high standards of our profession and always seek to correct any and all abuses within the automotive industry.

To uphold the integrity of all members of the Automotive Service Association.

About the Author

Russell McCloud was born in Fort Huachuca, Arizona. His family moved to Yuma when he was one year old, so he can legitimately claim Yuma as his lifetime home. He has two sons, Scott and Jeff, both of whom work in the family business. They have blessed him with three granddaughters and a grandson. In 2008, he married Joy, a girl he'd known since childhood but never gave him the time of day until they met again in 2006.

In 1997, Russell became involved with the ASA (Automotive Service Association) at the state level. He represented Arizona at the national level in the Affiliate Assembly for four years. He was then elected by his peers to serve on the ASA National Board of Directors from 2007 through 2010.

Russell has been a member of Fort Yuma Rotary since 1999 and has served three years as a board member. As a member of Fort Yuma Rotary, he has earned three Paul Harris Fellowships.

In 2001, he was accepted to Project CENTRL, a rural leadership program, and he is a graduate of class XVI. Because of Project CENTRL, he started a fund raising committee for Amberly's Place (a victim's advocacy and crisis counseling center) in 2002. The annual fundraiser, Amberly's Week In Paradise, brought in almost $60,000 for Amberly's Place in 2013. In 2003 he was invited to join the board of Amberly's Place where he has served as the board's President the last two years.

In 2004, he successfully ran for public office for the first time, winning a seat on the Yuma County Board of Supervisors. He was re-elected in November 2008 and again in November 2012.

In October of 2014, the same week this book was finalized, Russell was honored at the *Heart of Yuma* awards as Yuma's 2014 "Outstanding Leader" for his work with Amberly's Place. This book went to print on October 30th, one day after the 45th anniversary of Dennis McCloud's first day in business as Accurate Automotive Attention.

Notes

[i] Automotive Service Association. About Us/Our Story. http://www.asashop.org/about/our-story/. June 29, 2014.

[ii] Not Just Oil, Pennzoil. Learn About Motor Oil/Types of Motor Oil. http://www.pennzoil.com/learn-about-motor-oil/types-of-oil-and-recommended-use/. June 30, 2014.

[iii] United States Flood Loss Report. Executive Summary. http://www.nws.noaa.gov/hic/summaries/WY2012.pdf. June 30, 2014.

35441032R00067

Made in the USA
Charleston, SC
09 November 2014